Heart X-rays

A Modern Epic Poem

Marcus Colasurdo and G.H. Mosson

PMPRESS

PM Press PAMPHLET SERIES

0001: BECOMING THE MEDIA: A CRITICAL HISTORY OF CLAMOR MAGAZINE
By Jen Angel

0002: DARING TO STRUGGLE, FAILING TO WIN: THE RED ARMY FACTION'S 1977 CAMPAIGN OF DESPERATION
By J. Smith and André Moncourt

0003: MOVE INTO THE LIGHT: POSTSCRIPT TO A TURBULENT 2007
By the Turbulence Collective

0004: THE PRISON-INDUSTRIAL COMPLEX AND THE GLOBAL ECONOMY
By Eve Goldberg and Linda Evans

0005: ABOLISH RESTAURANTS: A WORKER'S CRITIQUE OF THE FOOD SERVICE INDUSTRY
By Prole

0006: SING FOR YOUR SUPPER: A DIY GUIDE TO PLAYING MUSIC, WRITING SONGS, AND BOOKING YOUR OWN GIGS
By David Rovics

0007: PRISON ROUND TRIP
By Klaus Viehmann

0008: SELF-DEFENSE FOR RADICALS: A TO Z GUIDE FOR SUBVERSIVE STRUGGLE
By Mickey Z.

0009: SOLIDARITY UNIONISM AT STARBUCKS
By Staughton Lynd and Daniel Gross

0010: COINTELSHOW: A PATRIOT ACT
By L.M. Bogad

0011: ORGANIZING COOLS THE PLANET: TOOLS AND REFLECTIONS TO NAVIGATE THE CLIMATE CRISIS
By Hilary Moore and Joshua Kahn Russell

0012: "VENCEREMOS": VÍCTOR JARA AND THE NEW CHILEAN SONG MOVEMENT
By Gabriel San Román

0013: ON COMMUNITY CIVIL DISOBEDIENCE IN THE NAME OF SUSTAINABILITY: THE COMMUNITY RIGHTS MOVEMENT IN THE UNITED STATES
By the Community Environmental Legal Defense Fund with an introduction by Thomas Linzey

0014: THAT PRECIOUS STRAND OF JEWISHNESS THAT CHALLENGES AUTHORITY
By Leon Rosselson

0015: DIVIDE AND CONQUER OR DIVIDE AND SUBDIVIDE? HOW NOT TO REFIGHT THE FIRST INTERNATIONAL
By Mark Leier

0016: HEART X-RAYS: A MODERN EPIC POEM
By Marcus Colasurdo and G.H. Mosson

0017: THE YOUNG C.L.R. JAMES: A GRAPHIC NOVELETTE
By Milton Knight * Edited by Paul Buhle and Lawrence Ware

0018: EVENTS AND VICTIMS
By Bartolomeo Vanzetti * Edited by Jon Curley

PM Press Pamphlet Series No. 0016
Heart X-rays: A Modern Epic Poem
Marcus Colasurdo and G.H. Mosson

ISBN: 978-1-62963-513-2

PM Press
PO Box 23912
Oakland, CA 94623
www.pmpress.org
www.pmpress.org.uk

Printed in the UK by Calverts
www.calverts.coop

HEART X-RAYS

Below the Tower

Out of the dream machine, far
from my parents' daytime haul, out
of these mirrory blank smiles, far even from
contraband nights of metamorphosis, unplug my sight;
out of the screaming pass & fail, no longer below salivating
billboards, beyond values bartered and sold, far
from the scramble for value, far away
from the famished addicted wired walkers
of the fattest cities, away from the obesity
of replicated sameness, utopia's five-dollar whores,
            release me toward
                        an elixir that nourishes
even men and women who anchor themselves
to encased hearts, whisk me past
oasis of freedom by shopping, past
where the shut-down towns are turned
into plastic and steel theme-parks;
            phoenix-heart soar
                        through less—quirky
                              and wobbly as any close friend—

What thin tower is this
and where are the magicians
among the lines at the monolith's foot?
I hear the people grumble, impatient,
sleepwalking through a chant
they barely recall. Whose ziggurat
winds up toward speechless skies?
The shamans have been slaughtered
            and the hum of their hints
blows a distant breeze

elsewhere. A nation of talkers
mobs airwaves with gossipy tongues—
        remote on—
        remote off—

Field

Dreams of underwear cannot hide my nakedness—

Always time for song.
Don't wait too long.
Teased by wind? Why pretend?
Listen. Birds praise
Alphabetless days
Of the sun's clock
Above the tick
Tock. Grassy toes,
Curled up nose,
Summer's rose.
Crying eyes
Of a lover's smile
Pause a while.
Invest my heart
For those cave days
Roseless
But not afraid.
Love, prevail
Amid the tales
Until words fail
For even you, dear,
Must burn and fade
(flare anew)
But not today.

Fade, song,
With autumn's long
Shalom to winter's
Shanti of snowfall.

Youth's the time to fly, why cry yourself
dry, slide to the beaches where sunrise
melts to sleeping bags full of wet and dark beginnings,
ride to the basketball court to dunk dreams, jet through
chattering cities, late-night parties, backroads, who knows?
You'll join us, soon enough, old men in closed rooms
where we decide where to sign the document
and to whom it must be mailed and copied,
inching the social wheel forward, comma by signature,
from "confirm the fact" to "confirmed fact"
as the kids dance around a mandolin of images.
From fire, life,
From experience, char,
From the char, knowledge,
From knowing . . . gardener.

Green desire, sustaining sun, take me too!
The universities employ paraplegics of the heart,
geniuses of computer programs and robotic bombs
who publish explanatory books that dwarf the wide world,
but I have drunk too much of light's fragrant pooling
on a summer sunflower's heavy head drooping
toward the good soil, yet erect and still waiting
in the bright meadow blaze for the symphony of bees
to be made so sober.

Wait, I have to check my iPhone.
I'm not your brother's keeper, but here, keep the change,
homeless dude, wasted hippie kid, hip slacker who clutches coffee

to stay awake. Bring in the big trucks, dozers,
huffing excavators, replace trees with box stores,
dig deep down and level.
Haul up the earth, thirty feet below, and process
it into component parts, sell colored gravel
for landscaping, and fill dirt to pack the cleared plots.
Let's frame another suburb, join us.
Use this coupon. Plant private gardens.
Call it yours. Where did the birds go?
Buy more. Who took the worms? Lock doors.

What did you do today, honey?
It's hard to describe, my duckling,
Everything I did can be fit into an idea.
O sweet spicy duckling, I fear I am fading.

Who wedged the universe into an alphabet
within a computer screen? Scroll through
all the way. My homeless heart cannot fit
into any safe deposit box. It just left town.

Look, here come the birds, here come the butterflies.
They land on fences, on starter trees.
They arrive.

Behind your tears,
The past, behind your
Past, this dirty web,
Behind each thread, ants
And spaceships, dinosaurs and
Hurricanes, a baby's smile,
A sky of feeling, swift flight
And beautiful falling.

Fuck the man and his motherfuckin' plan
Who I am? My mind goes back to Abraham
Understand—I ain't changed by brand names,
name games, sold lines, bought pain, time schemes,
dream chains—   not rearranged—
Put yr hands up & say, HEYYY!
                              Rhythm rooted
                                        Get to it
                                             Turn time
                                                  Into music
                              for there ain't no escape   from the mindscape
                                   Ain't too late   to dig deep and relate
                                        Don't wait   for
                              "Payday Holiday"—
                                                  "Gotta change the diaper"—
                                                                      "Pass the remote baby"—
Fuck the man and his motherfuckin' plan
Rewrite the scene
                    Ancient dreams!
                         Gotta scream
                              Baby-boo stay true
                                        If you bruise, search too—
                                                  Well, who loves you?
JAY-Z was a hero to most
but he never meant shit to me
selling the bling bling death race   CEO-mask tool-faced
money-strut circle chase   loud-noise light-blast
to erase   history   "for once a pimp,
always pusher—"
                              I don't need gold watches to tell the weather
Fuck the man and his motherfuckin' plan
How long will it take to understand?
Why make the golden calf loom larger?
I'm heading inward

Gotta be a dodger *Just holla!*
All in *no chaser* *Let's go!* *Get bothered*
Universal seeker
Mind slave never
Nevermind the sellers
Be your own weather
Fuck the man and his motherfuckin' plan
Shut off devices *Heal and get better*
Faith is a vision *Love through the never*

Street Scene

while you
are walking,
your head cradled
in your phone,
your ears plugged
with plastic,
there is no way
to alert you;
while you are
walking, cooing
to pictures of yourself,
there is no way
to warn you;
while you
are walking rectangled
into hypnosis,
you cannot see
me
waving my wild arms
from
this

upper floor
window—
but
beside you,
matching your stride
with familiar eyes,
the rapist
is
wearing
those
cool
shoes.

Charleston

after the shooting (June 17, 2015)

Tonight, I don't know which God
    you're praying to.
I can't tell which flag you salute.
I am not certain
    if you believe in ghosts—
but tonight, I hear them singing:
    Oh come, Oh come, Emmanuel
and I wonder just what
    the cemetery shovels are burying
tonight. Suppertime has long passed.
Can it be that the mouth
    of your port, Charleston, still tingles
with the taste of flesh in chains?
I hear the coded talk-talk
    and the magnolias sweat down
whispering that the hood and torch
can now be measured in gigabytes,

in radio screech, and the law
for some is a coloring book
crayoned with burnt flint,
yet still, they sing:
    Oh come, Oh come, Emmanuel
History imparts her lessons
only, it seems, to those
who still believe
in the learning.
The walk toward
wisdom routes
through Golgotha, indeed,
but arrows not
toward suffering
or so the long song
promises. If the mapmaking
of human minds
    learns from our hearts
elasticity . . . can you still think
    that the sun favors one
        and not the other?
For a century and a half, the nation's doors
have opened wider and wider. Tonight,
one hand is extended your way, though
        I do not know for how much longer—
as nearby
    and closer still
        another voice
            has joined the song.

Leaving the Gift Shop

I.
Let's commence the Literature of Me
It's so practical I'm endlessly fascinating
Even in the fascist army, anyone can write a memoir
That bum ranting on the corner doesn't get it, does he?
So what he had a vision as a fifteen-year-old hitchhiking on a highway.
His father didn't beat him anymore, did he? And he avoided butt raid
When he snuck away as the drunk snoozed off. That vision of G-d
Didn't include me, did it?

Blow this out yr ass, I'm back on stage!
In the Literature of Me, you'll weep when I weep,
Laugh when I laugh, go with me to Mom's house
For a reunion after a silent year. You too?
When did relationships become so hard?
Wait a second, I have to send a tweet and answer
Four emails. I need a soda. In the Literature of Me, I eat well
And don't gain weight. It's like a T.V. show.
Except, I'm the T.V. Get over yourself.
No clear glass window but just a front row seat.
And because it is loud and famous, don't you run and come?

II.
In practical cars with practical eyes, I don't
want to drive on practical roads toward practical goals.
Who are the old ladies thinking of shopping on Saturdays?
Will they readjust their wall hangings today with the retired man next door?
As we pass each other in opposite turning lanes, I X RAY this stranger
who putters today's freedom through errand
after errand and glimpse a low mist
about us with a faint strobing gray hue

like a living language and looking back at me
waiting with mute patience
for my allegiance under some vast flag.

III.
Techno-Human Poly-Trans-One
Facebooking the mothering void into insta-image
And history to infobite

Joe's heart shows up on the assembly line looking for a date:
Do you like poodles or bulldogs, noise rock or classical music?
Gotta go and accessorize the heart.
I can shake your hand or run you over it's such a crowd.

Sold the land to *TACO ABC*
Got a bunk bed at *123 FURNITURE*

Poly Trans Morph Reducto One
Twittering in front of invisible bird notes
Quote unquote the silence until it's deafeningly loud

Here I stand, with a bouquet of fragments
And a buried heart
And above it looms the mannequin and her atomic clock

IV.
Memo to File: If we turn the mystery into a tourist site, the people will stand in line even though they are lost. This way, Hollywood movies lead the way into longer lines toward roller coasters, and really, even I can't resist them. Kids aren't potted plants and someone has to occupy their engrossed eyes. Their parents are even worse because they dress in our identities. Identity for sale! Identity for sale!

V.
Where is the key if I am the prison?
If you are the key, how am I your jailor?
Can we uncage from this age-old lockstep
if I sing your song, and you sing mine?

Mother, I am not like your brother but also a teeny toy soldier.
Father, I am not you without the car accident and bad marriage.
Dad, can I grow as tall as your skyscraper heart buried in tears?
Mom, I want to help you dance naked among high school ghosts.

Let's create a path by clearing.
From the perspective of learning, everything can be good.
Let's dance the oldest dance of friendship.
A friend helps you sing around the fire and walk wounded on the road.

Let's call the road, time.
Let's call the journey, us.
Let's call the hints, maps.
Let's call the lesson, love.

Soul Kitchen

1.

All up and down
    the broad flanks of the Susquehanna,
on both sides of the muddy Mason-Dixon,
across state lines of mountain laurel and pine,
there's a work dance in progress:
a culinary creation
    gestating a brand new nation -
something aromatic being prepared
    in the kindhearted sculleries,

something fine and fresh
    being served up with soul.
Read the recipes, one and all!
    Something human is happening here.
These angels are necessary.

2.

And so, an idea began in one empty belly -
sound became word
and the word gurgled true
like a white-hot tattoo:
simple and terrifying,
choked and near broken,
the word whispered out
as a scream of exhaustion:
    Hunger.
And truly, it has been said
that the voices of the famished
are the last to be heard -
until the dead once again
sing clear as birds -
and towers of wealth
have crumbled to sand -
and stranger becomes friend
with the reach of a hand. . . .
        All who hungry, shall be fed
and the words became the work of nourishment;
and the words became the many who heard them;
and our dance began again.

3.

What a sight to see
this sharing by degree
in a sanctuary free

where hope demands no fee.
All kinds come through the welcoming door:
all colors, ages, languages
of the Lord. Sometimes, it seems
that my country's whole history
walks toward me
in the late afternoon light.

Some come off the windblown streets.
Some come empty out of silent rooms.
Some come grateful for their child's next meal.
Some come searching for that special one.
Some are veterans of economic war
carrying too many losses
    and too few wins.
Some seek merely
    to hear a voice besides their own.
Some come with their brains
    in fiery debate:
which bills to pay, which ones can wait.
Some have lost their future
    before it began: taken
by accident, taken by foreign conflict - taken
by the money changers, taken by slashed wrist
political pens - sucked up by syringe and rotgut -
taken by fire in the real estate night -
future pink-slipped on a black ice road -
lost in the gloom of the factory's last day -
Sometimes, when the world turns toward cold
        only one question remains -
            if the future is sold
                and hope has been repossessed
what exactly is left
    in the place called home?

Perhaps tomorrow expects us to answer its question.
Perhaps we have always known that.

4.

Indeed, I see notion turned into motion -
a moving circle of engaged energy
radiates out like karma in action:
50 pairs of hands in a mudra marvelous -
500 fingers efficiently flying -
a fandango of fabulous feet -
getting busy at the very burners
of home-cooked resurrection.

It's a blue-collar
blue-aproned ballet. . . .
It's a two-step peel and prep.
It's a mighty nice slice and dice.
It's a shimmy-shake boil and bake.
It's a three-course tour de force
with a salad to open -
and just exactly like you're hope'n,
there's *music* in *this* menu:

It's a meatloaf moonwalk
and a fried chicken cha - cha -
it's mashed potatoes and stewed tomatoes
and German-speaking coleslaw.
It's a righteous rumba of ravioli
and meatballs sauced aplenty -
down the street—it's 10 bucks a plate—
up here, it don't cost a penny.
It's taco tango, with beans cooked twice,
with salsa and cheese and jitterbug rice.
There's creole shrimp

    and pierogies in butter -
there's a man and woman
    kissing each other!
There's Bolshoi burgers
    and thick beef stew -
there's jambalaya and pasta fazool.
There's a ham that's hummin'
right off the bone -
plus greens and yams
from *way* down home!
There's carrots and celery
in a chicken soup waltz -
a clam chowdah too
that's low on the salt.
There's a line dance of pies
from apple to cherry -
key lime sublime
and a bowl of strawberries.
    More coffee?
    No problem.
Just let mc takc in
this dance of the sacred cooking fire,
this hand to table to mouth to belly
to deep soul satisfaction,
this mystical plate juggling.
Just give me one more minute
so I can become just as full up
where I feel my heart growing
again - spoon by fork -
aroma by aroma - just let me inhale this -
so I can remember where my truest nourishment
comes from.
Just
one

more
minute -
if you please;
and
while
you're waiting
maybe take a moment
for yourself.
Take a look around at
who's knocking
on your life's door,
waiting for you to open it again -
take a quick second for that, will you?
I'll be right back
with your coffee.

Send Comments Here

What do you have to add?
Don't lie, you've got the goods.
Please kindly write to:
Gotta find me—
(Who will arrive?)
((Selfie of a selfie?))
This too shall be a dead letter office.

Present— Past— Future—

—just clouds in the heart's sky—

Tense of Choice

Chesapeake Bay Haiku

Crow swoops low over
newly planted sorghum field -
food is everything.

Late night chicken truck
on empty country road -
I dream of slaughter.

Tomorrow morning:
fresh brown eggs, easy to find -
June sun warms the bread.

Hammer, home, some nails
can be all a person needs -
for now, rain can wait.

Waterman's radio -
anyone remember it?
Fiddle floats on high tide.

Heron skirts our creek -
wingspan greater than last glimpsed -
this heart follows her.

Guitar Repair

for Pussy Riot

Don't ask me how I know
but it takes a certain kind of passion
to go out looking for lightning
in the blind of the night.

Don't expect me to answer
your questions, I have spun past
any record paced to 33 and a third
with a music that lacks explanation.

Don't ask me to predict the weather
for it takes a certain kind of courage
to plug in a stolen microphone
in the middle of an ice storm.

Think you know me? I wanna invent
my own species. Better catch me on that mystery
train that's rollicking its way into town:
maybe early, maybe late—

to bust up minds or arrive on time—
but even so, all I know
is it takes a certain kind
          of skill

to grab the whip
from the jailer's hand
and use its lashes to restring
          a guitar.

Ringing the Bells

What is this tower
          that punctures the night?
Who built these songs
          wired wordperfect?

How does this candle
of blinking metallic light
transform to inhaled
auto-tuned dreams?
Who are the storytellers
that can give this grace?

Satellite's talk-talk
floats through the heartland.
A bordello beckons at reasonable
cost per minute.
The telephone mystic flashes
inches of gold.
As tell-alls out-tell all,
viewers channel-surf
for fattened wounds
with maggoty eyes.

Do you hear some bells, someone ringing them?
By the rivers of Babylon, we sat down
and how we wept, when we remembered. . . .

Whose courage of climbing
though lonely silence
brings about such sweet chiming?

Ring them bells
from the city, and how we wept . . .
requiring a song. . . .

Game On

I.
Because we signed up by being born, let's double down
and hold hands to wade into the screaming. You don't
hear it? I mean the aquifers of pain even while dancing
and deeper down than any day's puppet show, not shrugged
off like some stuffed animal almost won at the carnival
as you get "all adult" and see the strings of colored lights
as mere electricity. Oh, foolin' your friends? That poker face
can't sequester sunken tears. Try again, without the boredom mask.
Maybe suffering is just the comet
of time ripping off the mortal flesh by fire?
Yet the hawks circling Highway 83
this Thursday afternoon after work
spoke of a delicate dream. Come with me,
I've been stranded in masks
too. Let's leave behind the language
of pretending and enter
the mystery. Oldest Pal,
Silent One, what creature could give us
life not as an answer, but a question?
Well, YOU . . . but that solves nothing and
leads us to wonder about math.
The factory of human squirrels
keeps adding and subtracting
but one day the big breakthrough
will announce an infinity of silence
and wonder of how equations hold us.

II.
The last thing I wanted to do
in our relationship, darling,

was hurt you further so I left. I ran from you
to the snowy mountain only to find
the world reflected back to me through my pain.
I am a snake biting its own tail, many-headed,
O Lord, Inshallah, release me from this burning,
from this prism mirrored cave. Shalom coming, Shalom going, and
upon those words, a Sherpa boy with a satchel of my childhood,
photo album of my friends and enemies, diary
of my parents' wounded secrets, appeared
and handed me half the load
to shepherd us homeward.

The last thing I wanted was for you
to leave, though these wounds whispered to me at night
to let you go. I couldn't solve your childhood, dredge it up
whole. Who will solve mine now?
You fled, despite our bargain, called "love"
on uncertain tongues unsure what life might be
without knowledge of love. Now, alone, not destitute,
yet solid, I sing this song? And again, slowly,
I can see creeping around the corner
elves attracted to my song. Some skip and wink.
Others carry their loads. One smiles but runs off.
Again, my song makes me a home here
by leading others homeward.

III.
Banksy broke into this poem, tagged it up: Stop whining
and feed the starving kids, lean on the wall of injustice, see
the VIP disco party, exit through the gift shop. Not bad, and reasonably
priced, I thought to myself as I returned to the poem and plotted my escape.
Am I my brother's keeper? Excuse me,
not that question again. Art must be new, like plastic
turned into recyclable iPhones. You know, if

we kill each other with words, no one will know
because it happens so slow. That's so clever, let's
do it together. We may well win
a prize. Even if you can't take it with you,
maybe it will stick to a wall somewhere
like a new ancient name, aflame,
calling forth admirers, winking at
Death. Of course, Death knows,
but you don't, do you, lover
of stars and art, dancing
with Banksy and Pussy Riot,
where the key is for any locked door.
No it was never locked, was it?
The gift shop opens up.
You ran headlong into all that hurt you, so tempting.
But here, forget the disco ball, exit the gift shop,
duck though the kitchen where the food is scrumptious
and run until you're blank and free.

IV.

What is the difference between you and I?
        Ocean, I am here, let's open.
Shut the heart down.
        Why is my longing a rainbow
and where does it go?
        Coax the heart down.
Sea, bathe me in the lull of thinnest low tide.
        If I can't cure this rooted pain,
        can I disperse it into delicate rain?
            Shelter the heart now.
            Sand, with your billion hands, uphold this body.
If the love I feel turns my words to thunder,
        let the heart peek out.
            Waves, cradle me in your rhythm.

About the Authors

Marcus Colasurdo is the author of 11 books, including the underground classic novel *Angel City Taxi*. Over the years, he has worked as a bartender, boom microphone operator, waiter, taxicab driver, factory worker, Job Corps counselor, farmworker, journalist, construction laborer, teacher, and more. His explorations have taken him across the length and breadth of the United States, a significant part of it achieved through the lost art of hitchhiking. As a writer for the page and stage, Mr. Colasurdo also is the founder of Gimme Shelter Productions, a nonprofit organization of artists whose performances benefit homeless shelters, feeding programs, and other worthy causes. More recently, Mr. Colasurdo helped found Soul Kitchens in Baltimore, Maryland, and Hazelton, Pennsylvania, which provide free meals to those who need them with the goal of culinary panache and deep-rooted nourishment for all who come to eat, volunteer, and be present. Mr. Colasurdo hails from the anthracite coal country of Pennsylvania.

G.H. Mosson is the author of two books of poetry, *Questions of Fire* (2009) and *Season of Flowers and Dust* (2007). His poetry has appeared in *The Cincinnati Review*, *Measure*, *Smartish Pace*, and *The Tampa Review*; and has been nominated four times for the Pushcart Prize. He published the journal *Poems Against War: A Journal of Poetry and Action*, including the anthology *Poems Against War: Bending Toward Justice* (Wasteland Press, 2010). Mr. Mosson is a writer, lawyer, father, and dreamer. He practices employee rights and disability rights law as well as civil litigation. Over the years, he has organized for fair trade, not free trade, and for environmental conservation. With Mr. Colasurdo, he has performed as part of Gimme Shelter Productions. He has an MA from the Johns Hopkins Writing Seminars, where he was a teaching fellow and lecturer, and a BA in English. Mr. Mosson hails from NYC and lives in his second home state of Maryland.

Special Thanks

Craig O'Hara, for bringing this to light; PM Press, for your amazing gusto; Gerry LaFemina, for your expert edits; Jonathan Rowland, for your cover art and stupendous design; fellow artists and poets, past, present, and future, for your provocations and inspirations; our audiences, for your sharing; and to those in our lives, walking this road, you know who you are, thank you!

PM Press was founded at the end of 2007 by a small collection of folks with decades of publishing, media, and organizing experience. PM Press co-conspirators have published and distributed hundreds of books, pamphlets, CDs, and DVDs. Members of PM have founded enduring book fairs, spearheaded victorious tenant organizing campaigns, and worked closely with bookstores, academic conferences, and even rock bands to deliver political and challenging ideas to all walks of life. We're old enough to know what we're doing and young enough to know what's at stake.

We create radical and stimulating fiction and non-fiction books, pamphlets, T-shirts, visual and audio materials to entertain, educate, and inspire you. We aim to distribute these through every available channel with every available technology, whether that means you are seeing anarchist classics at our bookfair stalls; reading our latest vegan cookbook at the café; downloading geeky fiction e-books; or digging new music and timely videos from our website.

PM Press is always on the lookout for talented and skilled volunteers, artists, activists, and writers to work with. If you have a great idea for a project or can contribute in some way, please get in touch.

PM Press
PO Box 23912
Oakland CA 94623
510-658-3906
www.pmpress.org

PM Press in Europe
europe@pmpress.org
www.pmpress.org.uk

Friends of PM

These are indisputably momentous times—the financial system is melting down globally and the Empire is stumbling. Now more than ever there is a vital need for radical ideas.

In the many years since its founding—and on a mere shoestring—PM Press has risen to the formidable challenge of publishing and distributing knowledge and entertainment for the struggles ahead. With hundreds of releases to date, we have published an impressive and stimulating array of literature, art, music, politics, and culture. Using every available medium, we've succeeded in connecting those hungry for ideas and information to those putting them into practice.

Friends of PM allows you to directly help impact, amplify, and revitalize the discourse and actions of radical writers, filmmakers, and artists. It provides us with a stable foundation from which we can build upon our early successes and provides a much-needed subsidy for the materials that can't necessarily pay their own way. You can help make that happen—and receive every new title automatically delivered to your door once a month—by joining as a Friend of PM Press. And, we'll throw in a free T-Shirt when you sign up.

Here are your options:

- $30 a month: Get all books and pamphlets plus 50% discount on all webstore purchases
- $40 a month: Get all PM Press releases plus 50% discount on all webstore purchases
- $100 a month: Superstar—Everything plus PM merchandise, free downloads, and 50% discount on all webstore purchases

For those who can't afford $30 or more a month, we have **Sustainer Rates** at $15, $10 and $5. Sustainers get a free PM Press T-shirt and a 50% discount on all purchases from our website.

Your Visa or Mastercard will be billed once a month, until you tell us to stop. Or until our efforts succeed in bringing the revolution around. Or the financial meltdown of Capital makes plastic redundant. Whichever comes first.

Wisdom Teeth

Derrick Weston Brown

Foreword by Simone Jacobson
ISBN: 978-1-60486-417-5
$14.95

To consider *Wisdom Teeth* is to acknowledge inevitable movement, shift, and sometimes pain. There's change hidden just below the surface and, like it or not, once it breaks, everything has to make room. So goes the aptly titled debut poetry collection from poet and educator Derrick Weston Brown. *Wisdom Teeth* reveals the ongoing internal and external reconstruction of a poet's life and world, as told through a litany of forms and myriad of voices, some the poet's own.

Wisdom Teeth is a questioning work, a redefining of personal relationships, masculinity, race, and history. It's a readjustment of bite, humor, and perspective as Brown channels hip-hop, Toni Morrison, and Snagglepuss to make way for the shudder and eruption of wisdom.

> *"This brilliant first effort is akin to a mixtape, filled with nostalgic hip-hop references—MF Doom, A Tribe Called Quest, and J Dilla, among others—a love letter from a grown man still much enamored of the youth culture today. Found here are playful experiments with the eintou, bop, and brownku, African American forms seldom approached with such mastery."*
>
> —Simone Jacobson, managing editor for *Words. Beats. Life: The Global Journal of Hip-Hop Culture*

Late in the Day

Poems 2010–2014

Ursula K. Le Guin

ISBN: 978-1-62963-122-6

$18.95

Late in the Day, Ursula K. Le Guin's newest collection of poems, seeks meaning in an ever-connected world. In part evocative of Neruda's *Odes to Common Things* and Mary Oliver's poetic guides to the natural world, Le Guin gives voice to objects that may not speak a human language but communicate with us nevertheless through and about the seasonal rhythms of the earth, the minute and the vast, the ordinary and the mythological.

As Le Guin herself states, "science explicates, poetry implicates." Accordingly, this immersive, tender collection implicates us (in the best sense) in a subjectivity of everyday objects and occurrences. Deceptively simple in form, the poems stand as an invitation both to dive deep and to step outside of ourselves and our common narratives. As readers, we emerge refreshed, having peered underneath cultural constructs toward the necessarily mystical and elemental, no matter how late in the day.

The poems are bookended with two short essays, "Deep in Admiration" and "Form, Free Verse, Free Form: Some Thoughts."

> *"She never loses touch with her reverence for the immense what is."*
>
> —Margaret Atwood